He went to sea
in a thimble of poetry
without sail or oars
or anchor. What chance
do I have, he thought?
Hundreds of thousands
of moons have drowned out here
and there are no gravestones.

—Jim Harrison, "Poet Warning"

also by Diana Hayes:

Poetry:
Sapphire and the Hollow Bone (Ekstasis Editions, 2023)
Language of Light (House of Appleton, 2023)
Gold in the Shadow (Rainbow Publishers, 2021)
Labyrinth of Green (Plumleaf Press, 2019)
This is the Moon's Work (Mother Tongue Publishing, 2011)
The Choreography of Desire (Rainbow Publishers, 1999)
The Classical Torso in 1980 (Pulp Press, 1987)
Moving Inland (Fiddlehead Books, 1979)

Fiction:
Looking for Cornelius (Wipf & Stock/Resource Publications, 2025)

Drama:
Islomania: Saga of the Settlers (Salt of the Earth Productions, 1987)

HAWKING THE SURF

Diana Hayes

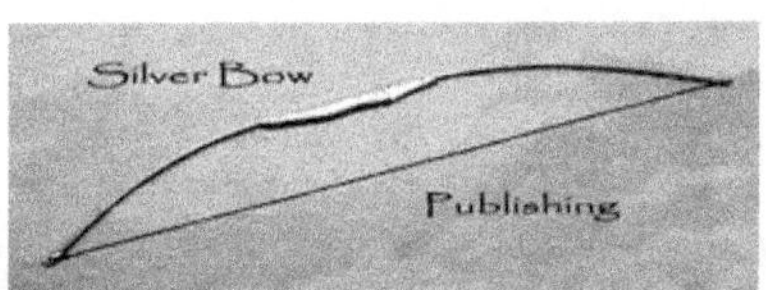

720 – Sixth Street, Unit # 5
New Westminster, BC
V3L 3C5   CANADA

Title: "HAWKING THE SURF"
Author: Diana Hayes
Cover Art: "Otter Point" photo by Diana Hayes 2022
Layout and Design: Candice James
Editor: Candice James

www.silverbowpublishing.com
info@silverbowpublishing.com
© Silver Bow Publishing 2025
ISBN: 9781774033890 book
ISBN: 9781774033906 e book

Library and Archives Canada Cataloguing in Publication Title: Hawking the surf / Diana Hayes. Other titles: Hawking the surf (Compilation) Names: Hayes, Diana, 1955- author. Identifiers: Canadiana (print) 20250310384 | Canadiana (ebook) 20250311682 | ISBN 9781774033890 (softcover) | ISBN 9781774033906 (Kindle) Subjects: LCGFT: Poetry. Classification: LCC PS8565.A88 H39 2025 | DDC C811/.54—dc23

to Clíodhna

*to make a little raft of words
on which they can make their way
to the other shore...
The return journey recreates the traveller*

Preface

Hawking the Surf is based on my immersion in the coastal landscape of British Columbia in the mid-1970s. I lived for a period on Vancouver Island's west coast, close to what is now the Juan de Fuca Marine Trail. Those early years and experiences informed much of my writing while completing an undergraduate degree at the University of Victoria. The poems in *Hawking the Surf* draw from my journal entries and a correspondence that I kept with B.C. writer and historian, the late Charles M. Lillard, who mentored my studies between 1975 and 1978. The poems also draw on my reading of seminal poets such as Robinson Jeffers, W.S. Merwin, and Saint-John Perse. You will find quotations from Lillard's poetry in italics in several of the poems. Detailed references are provided in the acknowledgements.

The Saddest Creatures on Earth focuses on current themes and concerns for the world that deeply preoccupy me. These poems traverse the cycles of grief, loss, hope, family, connection, the abundance offered in the natural world and how we must strive to protect it. The section ends with a return to old journal entries when I wrote my graduating paper on the work of poet and painter, P.K. Page. I spent many an afternoon at P.K.'s home, interviewing her and absorbing the wisdom she shared in her garden, getting lost in her paintings and mandalas which hung on the walls of her living room. She introduced me to the work of Loren Eiseley and the Sufi practitioners and poets that were central to her library. I was twenty-one and my senses were infused with her openness, her mystical eye, her calm radiance.

Photography has always provided a visual accompaniment to my poetry. Sometimes the images dance with the words before the ekphrasis process begins, and sometimes it is the other way around. My images in this collection are offered as a pairing and are part of the territory while I'm immersed in the intuitive process of writing poetry.

Table of Contents

Part I   Hawking the Surf / 9

Part II   The Saddest Creatures on Earth / 45

Photographic Interpretations:

PART I

Hawking the Surf

It was the year of leave-taking, erosion of sandstone
a shoreline falling away from the arms of Otter Point.

Otter Point Squalls   48°23′1.68″ N, 123°47′46.32″ W

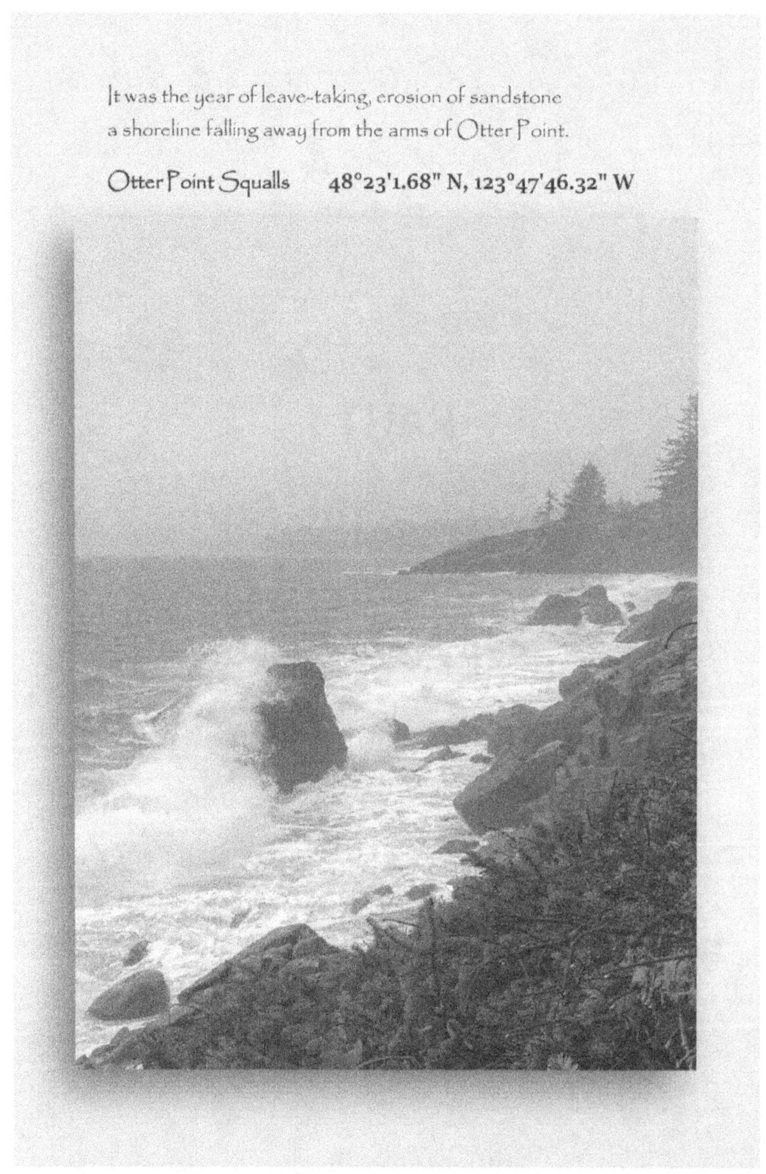

Otter Point Squalls
48°23'1.68" N, 123°47'46.32" W

It was the year of leave-taking, erosion of sandstone
a shoreline falling away from the arms of Otter Point.

That time the bluffs at Orveas were awash
squall after squall those late evenings in August.

Not the lazy glass-water days at Tugwell Creek
when we feasted on the endless catch.

You watched as I swam out to the invisible buoy
pulled myself out before slack tide turned

ran back to the cabin all saline and thirsty
and you, building a moat of silence with single malt.

I'd already written you out of my journal that spring
when you scribbled a note, asking for more time

like we could amble forever then lurch to avoid the crash.
Time weighs less than a squall of crows, you said in a poem.

Two full moons close enough to call perigee,
pulling us this way to that, testing the limit of tides.

I want to kill this distance, you wrote, *hawk the surf*
here on a jostling sea, the squall line pitching without end.

...I'm back at Ogden Point tracking your steps,
Watching three ravens tilting in the thermals

Deathwatch at Ogden Point   48°25'05" N, 123°23'17" W

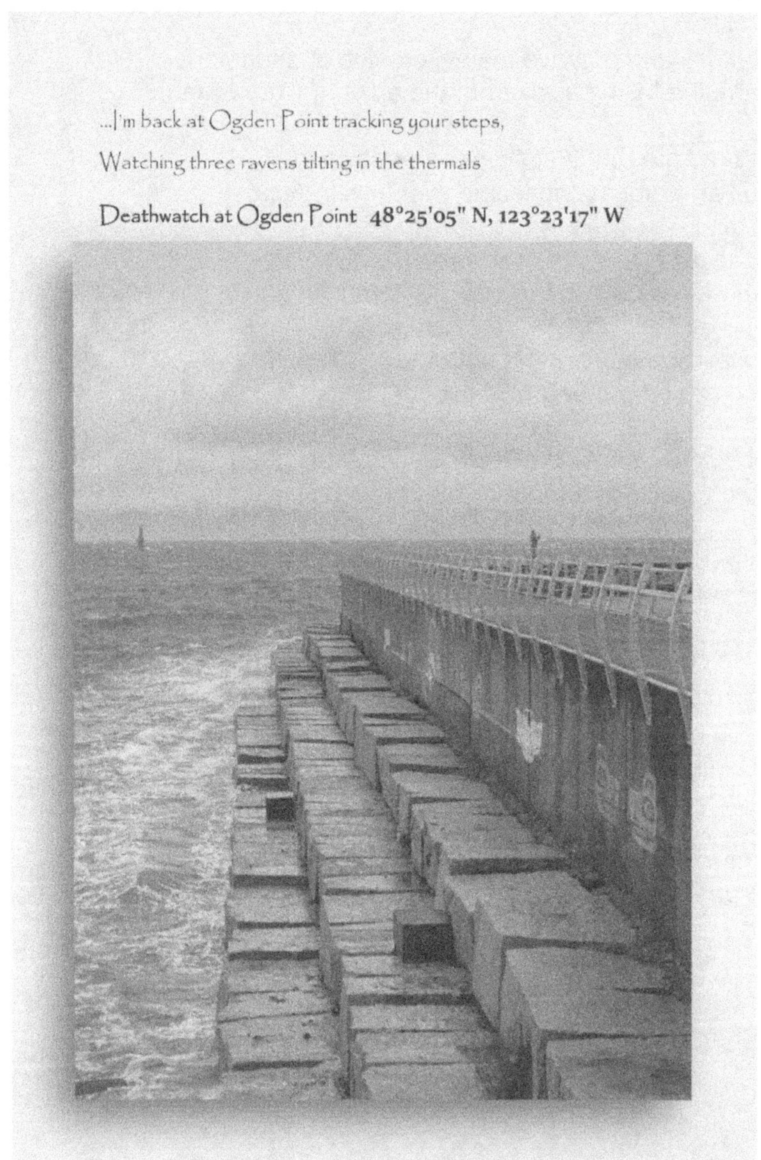

Deathwatch at Ogden Point   48°25'05" N, 123°23'17" W

I'm back at Ogden Point tracking your steps
watching three ravens tilting in the thermals

three lines scribbled and now faint
intonations lifting between stanzas—

that night the pilot boat circled, circling past
the occulting light, out in torrent waves

a child's handmade mittens and Lily doll
tossed in a tantrum, the tiny red dress bobbing

while the breakwater shuddered a tempest howl
I walked and paced with no moon to navigate

my undoing had little to do with gales
or fright but caught by Mesmer's spell

I shouted for a Kisbee ring, the ketch *Astral* long departed
from her berth, tacking past Neah Bay and Tatoosh—

a note tucked between pages, memory's deathwatch
now a dream's reach in a following sea.

Looking in the Margins
48°29'44" N, 123°42'44" W

Where have I been these mornings
scouting stones, tracing maps

not by the den's cozy hearth
lit up and slow-burning—

memory of an old shake roof under moss
this journal's sleight-of-hand

amulets and antlers on the mantel
another day awash in the scent of cedar

old Leechtown where I waded in a dream
sipped cool water in the margins

the bowl's rim and my thirst attuned
an ouzel's burbling medley of song

water-walker with feathered oars
diver on the brink of a stream

the old trestle's coordinates lost
heavy with nostalgia and the scent of gorse—

Oh sleep, come back to the roost
I am all fog falling beyond the water.

My Journal Falls Open to the Lake
48°28'34" N, 123°28'00" W

Late August's rumpled pages
the edge of memory's symmetry—

Prior Lake decades ago
words cast in silhouette

how the basking light
slipped low through emerald boughs

painted the evening in gold pastels
no hurry to erase the hour or day

no breath of wind to whisper
the lake's mirror mute

tepid at the ebb of summer
bare-skinned in fecund air

lean body diving
deep in that rust-hued water

a blue heron startled
crescendo of raspy squawks—

my journal nearly lost
remembering.

Postcards from the Skeena
54°14' N, 130°17' W

You'd been gone for weeks out beyond *Cape Nowhere*
leaving no tracks or signs, not holding out for the weather

no thought for a smooth landing, fishing and drinking
from that bottomless tumbler, Jameson's neat

your Drum rollies and yellowed fingertips telling me
you'd be happier in the north, the lure of a river's promise

still standing watch for Elena, how you changed
her name over the decades, her grip identical

postcards sent from Port Ed's general store
haphazard, not far from the Skeena's mouth

you'd returned to that river early like Chinook
a smolt in the belly of the salmon you'd said

survival wearing silver scales, a wallet full of flies
your last message dredged by kids on shore—

*The ground swell will break and rise, scudding
the heron's low flight. If I am wrong, I'm wrong.*

Postcards from Sitka
57°03'12" N, 135°20'05" W

It was July all summer. You'd taken a post north.
Sitka's fine arts camp, painting Bashmakoff in words,

stealing afternoons to trek the Cross Trail
up to Indian River Falls in day-long-light,

eleven miles out and back, muck boots and shirtless
mist floating the river's tableau, *The Sisters* stalwart.

Mary Ida in camp that year teaching mixed media
the mystery of fire trees calling her vision deeper,

beacons for mariners, preserving fire for heat—
Tlingit, Haida, Tsimshian stories told.

Today you walked the cemetery, two centuries old
the graves mostly hidden, smothered in devil's club.

Headstones from the ballasts of Russian ships.
The tomb of the princess without a name.

Last night you dreamed a mournful wail and tremolo,
a Great Northern Loon in the fall of night. West by North.

I Have Returned to the River
48°22' N, 123°50' W

I have returned to the river
never mind how long it's been

up to my thighs in memory now
and the water's lip as I wade out

not knowing if you reached the north bank
I could be lost in your book of days

feel the lap of river's last run
how it nudges clean and clear

I am further along than I charted
keeping still, waiting for the rocks to bite.

*

We spent that afternoon by the potholes
taking turns slipping from the grassy ledge

you packed a rusted winch in mid-day sun
sweat-drenched, hungry for salt

the old trestle a roadmap
making the long trek easier.

*

The night the earth moved the Richter scale
rumble and roar in feral pitch

tamed by the whiskey you poured
in twos near the open flame saying

it must be the dogs that strange earth's growl
a lowly mumble as cedars glance free of the panes

I did not get up to check the tidal surge
or stanchion the rogue years
or call out your name.

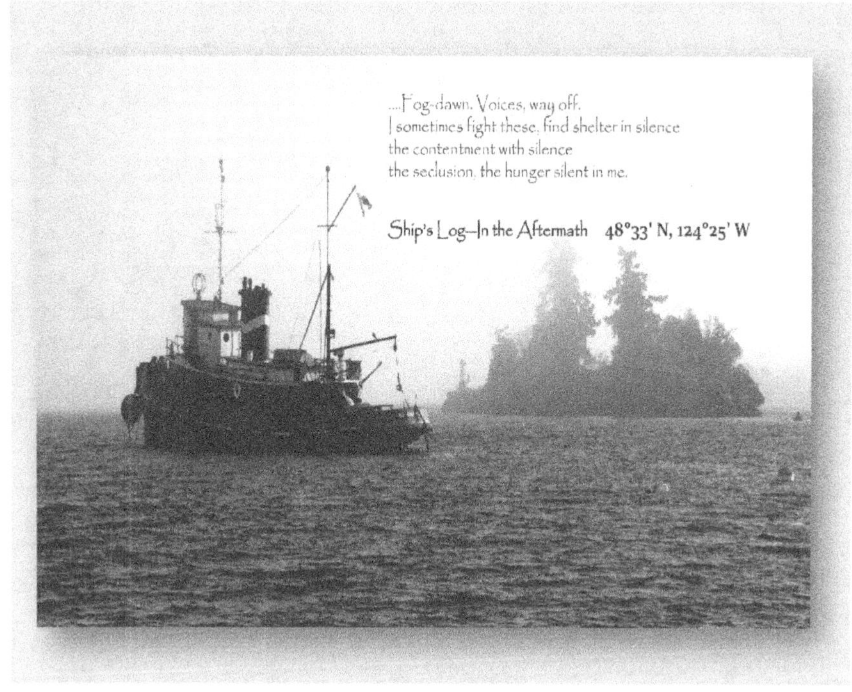
...Fog-dawn. Voices, way off.
I sometimes fight these, find shelter in silence
the contentment with silence
the seclusion, the hunger silent in me.

Ship's Log—In the Aftermath   48°33' N, 124°25' W

Ship's Log—In the Aftermath
48°33' N, 124°25' W

Troller's lumbering hull, me
an instrument marking time
the stench and labour of fish.

*

Fog-dawn.
Voices, way off.
I sometimes fight these,
find shelter in silence
the contentment with silence
the seclusion, the hunger
silent in me.

*

July.
The moon's pull
not to be trusted.
I have watched the fish carefully,
seen their slow death
in the waning.
One night soon
this moon will cross
your skiff's invisible wake.

*

July, still.
How one becomes lulled
by waves of summer's heat.
I was an errand in the long evenings.
Look at the signs—the grain in the wood
of your smile
designs disguising time
who's to ever be expert at this?

*

Imagine this condition:
the silvered fish convulse
again, on this wet day's deck.
In the night I can hear only
the slow movement of gills.

*

Imagine time
just like that.

Harris Point   56° 5′ 55″ N, 101° 13′ 30″ W

23

At Harris Point   a siege of rain   perpetual waves   the
woman wedged in this weather trap   with nothing but
fried smelts   and the fire-sheen   beyond   a river's long
turning.   For three days now   the tide slapping the surf's
bitter fist   against   her protected verge   flooding her
thoughts   with bull-kelp and salt   flooding her camp
as if she was   the prisoner and the bait.   She has only
herself   to contend with now   the days   a prophecy
she cannot tell.

Phone Call from Orveas
48°22' N, 123°50' W

I grip the wall phone, cold receiver   like it was your
arm, press it   tight against my ear   *you alright*, I
repeat   hearing your airy voice   out beyond the
middle distance   the quarrels and nautical miles
afraid to say the things   we need to hear   scrawled
words   instead in scattered   notebooks   reading
lines or memory   like we had never been estranged
behind window's beveled glass   holding you back
from the sheer rock fall   isobars shifting   waves
impatient at the door   while surf crawls the length   of
Tugwell's shore   asking   *how long has it been*   this
shadow-walking   the stone stairway down and down
I want to ride above the wind   and you dug in   with
your elemental nature and sea-blue eyes   checking
ferry departures   wrestling with uncommon sense
jagged breathing between pauses   white noise on the
phone's party line   you whispering *why are we so far
away   and you not here in my arms?*

Telegram from Rivers Inlet
51°41' N, 127°15' W

I want to kill this distance—from the long end of a too-dark silence—here with wind-logged spruce, cedar dolmen, wolf tree—love's a type of masonry built like old houses or this quay—stone upon stone.

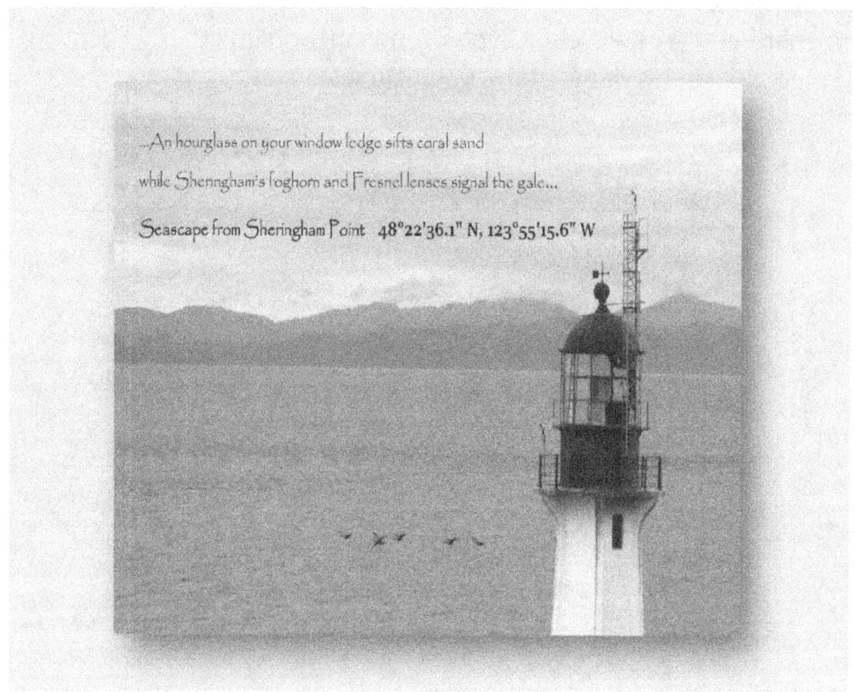
...An hourglass on your window ledge sifts coral sand
while Sheringham's foghorn and Fresnel lenses signal the gale...
Seascape from Sheringham Point   48°22'36.1" N, 123°55'15.6" W

Seascape from Sheringham Point
48°22'36.1" N, 123°55'15.6" W

Silence, like language, is best fit
for prayer and is the better half of both.

An hourglass on your window ledge sifts coral sand

while Sheringham's foghorn and Fresnel lenses signal the gale.

Here the *Anna Barnard* wrestled rock before her captain
        swam to shore.

Here five seamen climbed the bark's mast, clung to rigging
        until the tide went out.

These are your landmarks, Saint-John Perse's *Amers*
        beside the hearth

Seamarks in translation, long passages recalled until
        the barometer rose:

laid at your side, like the oar in the bottom of the boat...

        and the sea itself our vigil, the salty night bears us
        in its flanks...

Go more gently, loosen the clasp of arms, listen to the sea

Etched through panes of fog, our questions dissolved in silence

the blue halo of winter stars shone down from the Pleiades.

Westing in from rainforest inlets your Kynoch ravens tip and tuck

flip and chase, proclaim their *tok* and *kraa kraa* liturgy.

Winter Solstice at Barrow — Utqiaġvik
71°23'20" N, 156°28'25" W

Daylight reappears in the disguise of featherless birds.
You dream of migration.

I have considered the rough edge of your voice
the slow flight of your words

the tattered rhythms of your wings
and this I know:

sixty-seven days of darkness at the North Slope
next to the Beaufort Sea—the snowy owl remains.

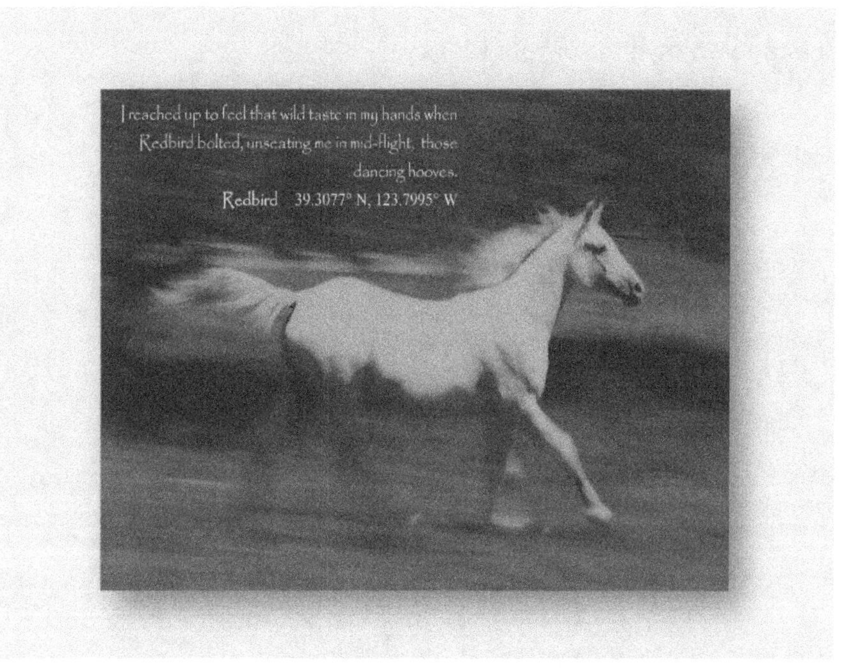
I reached up to feel that wild taste in my hands when
Redbird bolted, unseating me in mid-flight, those
dancing hooves.
Redbird   39.3077° N, 123.7995° W

Redbird
39.3077° N, 123.7995° W

On the road trip south, Highway 1 down Mendocino way
a Paschal moon over the clapboard cabin
                derelict on the cliffs near Cleone

It was here at Ricochet Ridge I asked the wrangler
                for the red roan gelding
his name Redbird like the book matches from Mission
                northern cardinal, all fire.

He started out gentle, an easy gait with light touch and snaffle
his mane pure silk flowing in sea-mist curls,
                my hands caressing
                the braided reins of supple leather.

Warm sweet sweat rising from his withers as we loped down
the trail to Ten Mile Beach but first past Inglenook Creek
                and the heirloom orchard

where apples ripened to crimson globes in ocean air,
I reached up to feel that wild taste in my hands
                when Redbird bolted
                unseating me in mid-flight, those dancing hooves.

I rested then on a rocky berm of beach drift when the shadow
of a steed appeared, wraith-like through family fields in
hames and traces his sire's bloodlines and blaze.

Redbird now in the surf following mares' tails like an Aughisky
amphibious water-horse persuading me, bare-breasted now
                into the raptor's wave

where the deep cool dark endless weight of water drew me
                down and down—
                as Harrison sang in his *Walking*: timeless place
                between kingdoms and the sea.

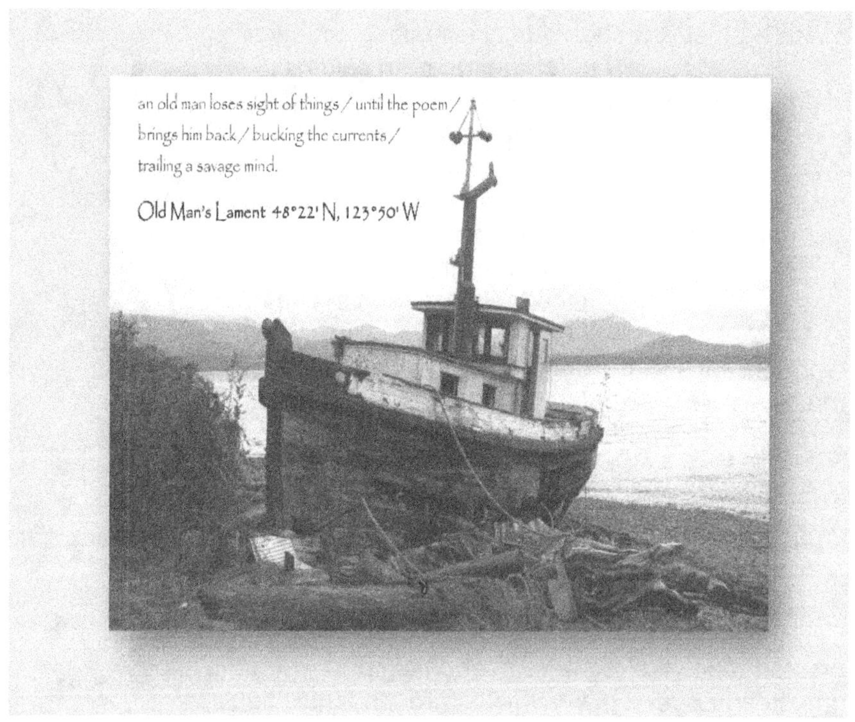
an old man loses sight of things / until the poem /
brings him back / bucking the currents /
trailing a savage mind.

Old Man's Lament 48°22' N, 123°50' W

Old Man's Lament
48°22' N, 123°50' W

what can be salvaged in a day /
rockweed and stone /
green glass globes /
wasen fishers / keeping droplines
afloat / my craft unmoored / drifting
leeward / me onshore / remembering

in a year from now what I've spoken /
will not be found in a tossed and
ragged / book of letters / illegible /
buried in sea wrack /
and bad weather

summer now / too much time has passed /
Juan de Fuca's coastline /
flotsam and bones /
no one to see my skiff spilling /
out beyond a neap tide

once I was persuaded by this
particular /curve of cobble beach /
what I spotted floating /
could be salvaged with my hands /
my past evades me

I should not have been a man /
with a fancy for words /
meddling in what slips / beyond
the years / memory shrouded in ink

an old man loses sight of things / until
the poem / brings him back / bucking
the currents / trailing / a savage mind

voices carry between mountains /
snow-capped peaks / now melting /
waves all day resolved in dying /
silence / without ripple or conundrum

I can't recall the message /
my last entry in the log /
something about a riddle / the day
has been / something in verse /
a poem / for August's blue moon

plea of earth-songs /
a prayer composed and folded
in the bottle / here I stumble /
words lost /out past my own message

From Merwin's Mountain
20°43' N, 156°10' W

Only on the rarest occasions, when the blue air,
Though clear, is not too blinding...

do I set off, the sky an indigo
my mother painted in a dream, taking with me

only the verse from an antique book, the fabric
of a shawl that draped not only my mind

but shoulders as I pressed down against the years
of blindness pretending colour, melancholy merging

in coral beads that fell at my feet as I walked deeper,
determined not to listen to the charms of the mountain.

It was you who finally spoke from a book of hours
clearly, but only once, saying: *reach beyond the luminous*

I am your house of refuge. Offer your hand not your glove,
I am with you now, although you do not know it

and so I became your companion, laying a fire
when my eyes needed a bridge between seeing and knowing,

when my hands held only syllables of thought gone to dust.
How I could see in the night's myriad reflection

a gate that became the mountain, how I had reached
the summit only in time to encounter my own image

beyond the bright and fleeting horizon.
Did you not tell me all those years ago

with a gait that you acquired from the talus slope,
that I would come back from the years of disbelief,

a stranger to my silhouette, feeling the braille stones,
the night that whispered from your ribs.

Now, I turn back the history that persists,
your words sounding a choral edge,

the prayer bell calling me down,
at last, from the mountain.

....amongst the impossible burden of rock,

wind clutching with sea-cold fingers

Hawking the Surf   36°32'31.5" N, 121°55'56" W

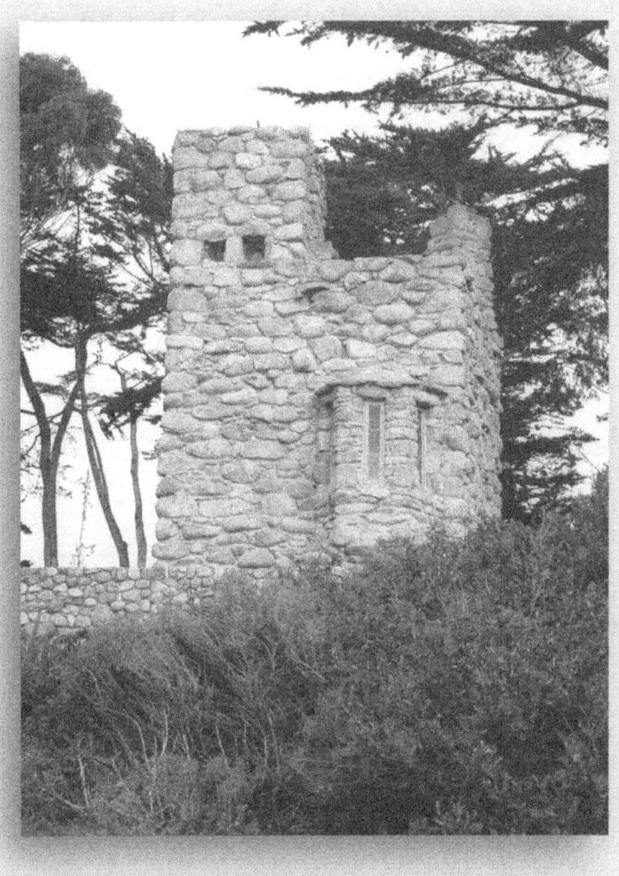

Hawking the Surf
36°32'31.5" N, 121°55'56" W

Among stones and quietness
The mind dissolves without a sound

You died young, wheeled out headfirst,

so a friend revealed in a letter.

I was travelling south that winter to Jeffers' Tor House

      Carmel-by-the-Sea

with a map you had drawn

by the dirge fire's flame at Otter Point

that same Pacific roar, granite stones piled along the ridge

your copy of Jeffers' *Tamar* in my satchel,

read aloud at Lone Cypress

amongst the impossible burden of rock, winds clutching

      with *sea-cold fingers*

Jeffers' hands calloused as yours, building Hawk Tower

one stone upon another, burning off afternoons

      to clear the darkness from his poet's desk

Una telling him to be with the sea air and masonry each day, needing the tactile to shake from his wild mind

      the carcass of Caldwell's mare in the surf

and later, Tamar's visage and nakedness where the stream

      made a pool

her kiss cold as winter stone, auburn hair trailing the water's

      translucence—

there are more stones than stories,

 impossible burdens buried in rock

and grass now grows where the flame flowered.

Meet Me Here
48°46'41" N 123°36'52" W

You must wait closer to dusk
measure the light between fingers

as it slips behind the ridge
Tzouhalem's crooked peak

and shadows fade
hoarding light on the west slope

be sure you've packed well
rations for the days to come

don't be surprised
when sheets of rain

slap no warning
squalls that move

like the sudden pitch
of your old man's skiff

when in that darkness
of northern winter

you fetched bait at Loy's
corner store in Ketchikan

a boy thinking you were
a man, a man of the sea

while ice crystals formed
on your knuckles and you bailed

your dory and tears froze
before they tattled on your fright.

This mountain is genius
clever twists every which way

leading to the summit
or not, hiding what can't be mapped.

I will be halfway along the scree
slow fire ready

the smoke will tell
plenty of time to set our camp

counting sundogs that mark time
confound the distance

you will like it here, it is all
we really have.

how it dogged us, that shadow hunter—
deep menace, ancient argument, a fatal wound
how the waterfall washed our trepidation
made us forget the mountain—

Bridging the Whitewater   49.32°N, 124.56°W

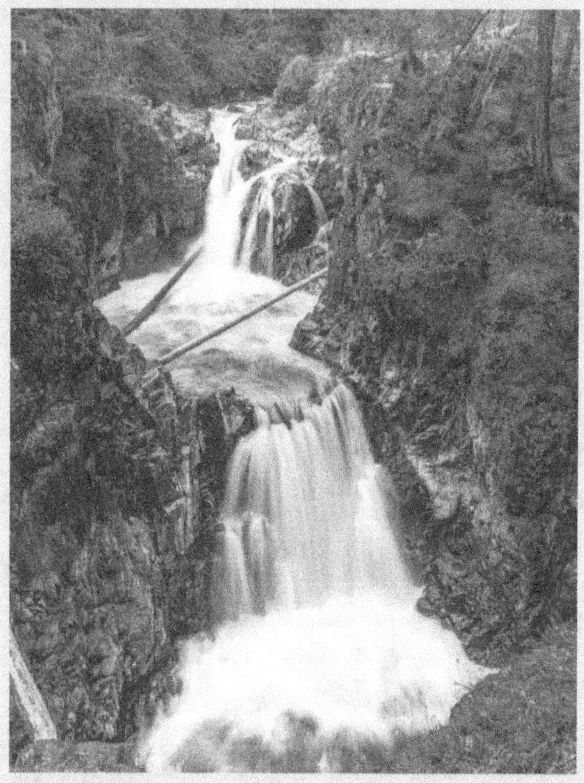

Bridging the White Water
49.32°N, 124.56°W

The mountain rests on the earth.
Its position is strong only when it rises
Out of the earth broad and great
Not proud and steep.
> The I Ching, Book of Changes, #23

We hiked the loop
Little Qualicum Falls, late afternoon

November light casting
hexagrams in fog

old growth quiescent on Wesley Ridge
east of the Cameron trestle

Mount Arrowsmith hidden from view
we did not see a figure, sullen

silent in trees, the spectre there
until we crossed the white-water bridge

how it dogged us, that shadow hunter—
deep menace, ancient argument, a fatal wound

how the waterfall washed our trepidation
made us forget the mountain—

at home, we prepare for winter
put in hay bales, wood piles

feeding fire from the earth
we hold stillness, our blessing now

far from the shadow's edge

PART II

The Saddest Creatures on Earth

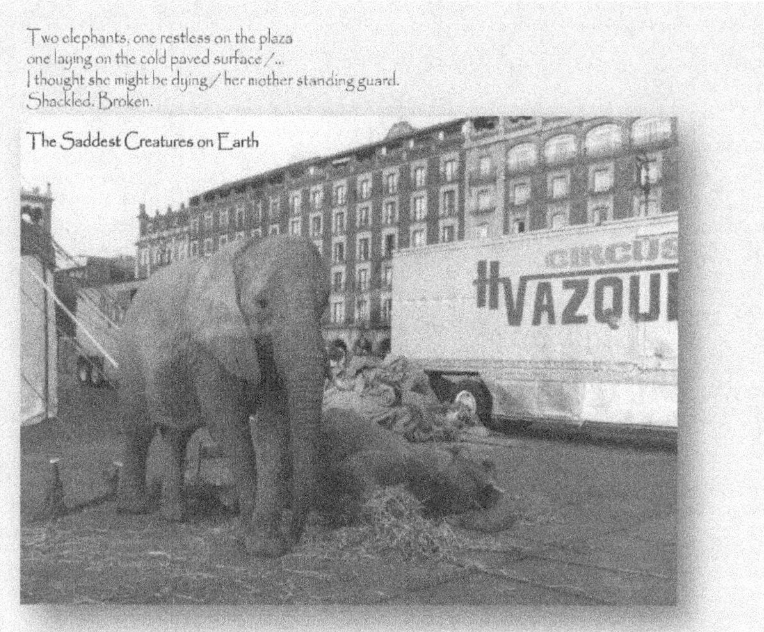
Two elephants, one restless on the plaza
one laying on the cold paved surface /...
I thought she might be dying / her mother standing guard.
Shackled. Broken.

The Saddest Creatures on Earth

The Saddest Creatures on Earth

> *...They mistake*
> *broken for feral, lonely for beautiful.*
> *These human hands that meticulously*
> *break nature to fabricate wonder.*
>
> Marie Metaphor Specht

i.

After I read your poem, *Don't Know Wild*
I climbed up onto the elephant's back
rode her to the end of the city limits
limitless sprawl and smog, farther along
to the edge of Old Popo, smoking mountain
past park trails, past *no entrada* signs
disregarding the guardian of parks and *Rurales*
their gesticulating arms, *gilipollas* they shouted
not wanting to mess with a pachyderm
      the spirit animal of peace.

But first I must speak of the winged migrations.
I was trekking to Rosario that year,
the monarchs' overwintering grounds
high in the Sierra Madre, mother of mountains
pine and oyamel forests that Aridjis saved
his poem praising the diaphanous life:
like a winged tiger, burning as you fly
air thin and silent, ten thousand feet above the sea.

Fragile, clustered, butterflies sleep
from November to March.
Those who had not made it out by spring
littered the trail, carcasses of orange and black
carpets of brittle wings under my feet.

ii.

I returned to the Hotel Majestic
on the edge of the capital's Zocalo
Aztec city of Tenochtitlan
once a centre for ceremony
ritual dance for nature, their gods
I was full of wonder, weary from the altitude
and the monarchs' soporific spell.

I woke to the sound of hammers clanging on metal
workers all night erecting tents and enclosures
makeshift scaffolds, transport trucks
backfiring in the laneway
hauling the saddest creatures on earth.

Two elephants, one restless on the plaza
one laying on the cold paved surface
a scattering of hay for a bed
small, likely a yearling, I thought she might be dying
her mother standing guard. Shackled. Broken.

iii.

This is how I left the country, carpets of dead butterflies
elephants confined for entertainment in tents
their ancient memories still roaming the savanna
cries and rumbles, snorts and calls
          trumpeting alarm.

Now I'm the rider gone rogue, dreaming
back at the edge of Old Popo
elephants roaming the grasslands
never again bowing to ringmasters
never tethered or chained.

She moved in a tight circle along the foggy waterline,
then made her dash to freedom, instinct's compass,
the endless ripple and surge of Pacific Sea.

Three Haibun for the Northern Fur Seal

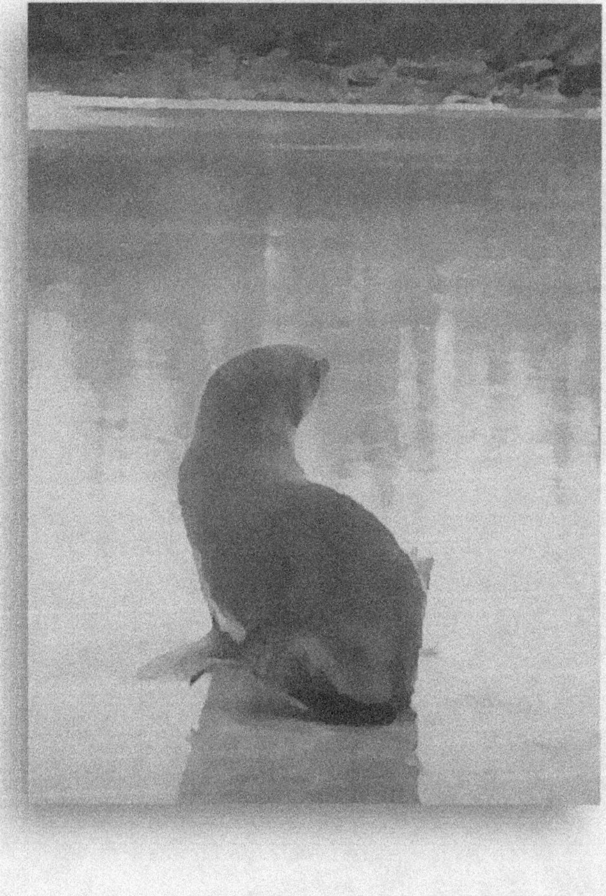

Three Haibun for the Northern Fur Seal
Lost

February, 54.3° N., unseasonably warm, the greatest number of days with rain. How many nautical miles had she travelled from the Pribilof Islands only to haul out on Prince Rupert's docks. Warming seas, colonies of toxic algae. Squid, sand eels, herring do not survive to keep her fed and alive. Sentinel seal, sensitive to any disturbance in her open-water world of salt and currents. Now lost, landlocked. Wandering the town's streets, humans gawking. Her fore flippers still strong enough on pavement, she walks then runs on all fours. Emaciation severe, dehydration, pneumonia setting in. Less than half the weight for her age and not yet a yearling. Too weary to vocalize, near-dead seal walking to her town street gallows.

February rain
burns molten holes in the ice.
Surrender falls through.

Rescue

Two plane rides, a coastal ferry crossing, a pickup truck carries her to the sanctuary and maternal hands of Marielle. Her species designated as *depleted* by the Mammal Protection Act: warming waters, melting ice, algal blooms, El Niño, human interference, colossal plastic eddies. Call recognition during nursing is essential for mums and pups. She growls, snorts, barks in her rescue bassinet. They feed her squid, shrimp-like krill, Walleye Pollock. Fatten her up. Heal the wounds. Months of separation make no difference to a mum. Her pup's calls are unmistakable. Bring her home.

Are you lost again?
Your calls ring through to my bones.
I know you by heart.

Release

April 14th, Long Beach, 49.15° N., Pacific Rim's
unobstructed path to the deep sea. Home waters
to female Northern Fur Seals on their migration
between Alaska and California. She graduated to
her outdoor pool at the sanctuary in time for
spring equinox. Took in whole fish, grew fat and
feisty for her journey, the final drive out to the
coast. She hesitated on that stretch of
windblown beach, looking back to her
surrogates. She moved in a tight circle along the
foggy waterline, then made her dash to freedom,
instinct's compass, the endless ripple and surge
of Pacific Sea.

The sea is my blood.
Waves carry me home again.
Praise my salty kin.

*Note: This poem is based on a true rescue of a Northern Fur Seal
that took place over a decade ago. The rescue mission was
coordinated and carried out by the Island Wildlife Natural Care
Centre, Salt Spring Island. Following successful medical
treatment and wildlife rehabilitation, the seal was released at
Long Beach in Pacific Rim National Park Reserve on the west
coast of Vancouver Island. The release was filmed by the rescue
team and has had over 700,000 views to date.*

Now, leaning into hospice times
we read one more poem for the night:
snow, *the way it forgives transgression*
a clear passage, leaving *no room for despair.*

Reading with David in Hospice

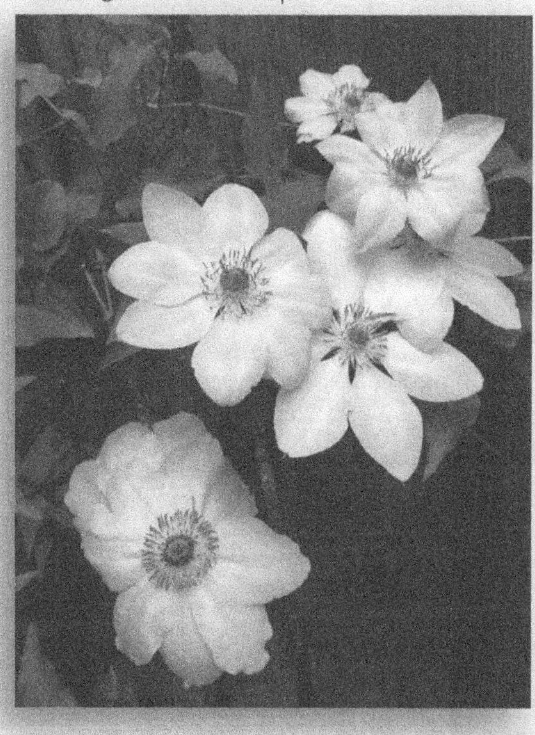

Reading with David in Hospice

You, the blue-eyed rider in the night
who can see reflections flicker and glow
not the whiteouts on Great Slave Lake
but in Patrick's *Winter*—book of loss and endurance.

Here in late spring's twilight, we call up
fields of fireweed in the Barrens
mountain avens and cloudberries
carpets of crimson welcoming all the senses.

Now, leaning into hospice times
we read one more poem for the night:
snow, *the way it forgives transgression*
a clear passage, leaving *no room for despair.*

After Patrick Lane's "Winter 1",
from Winter, Coteau Books, 1990

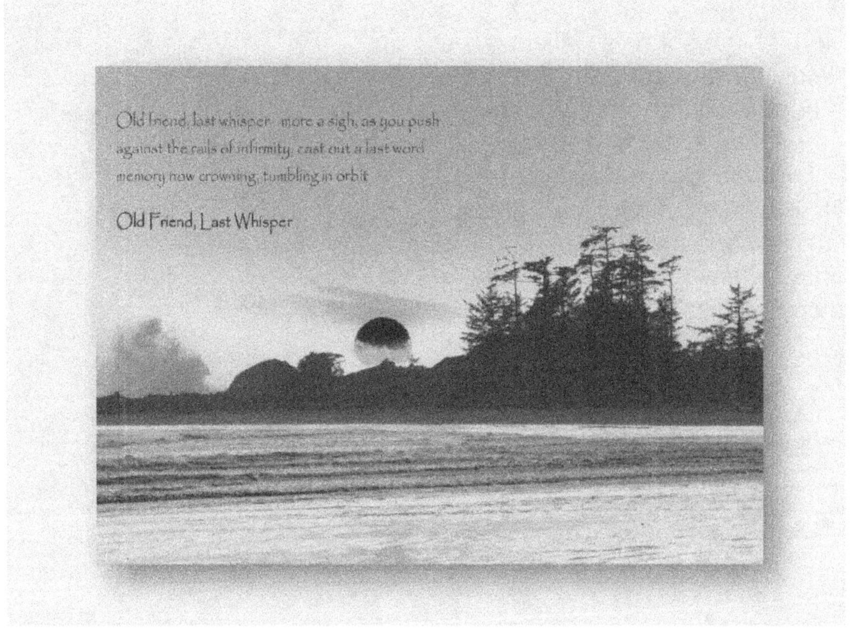
Old friend, last whisper more a sigh, as you push
against the rails of infirmity, cast out a last word
memory now crowning, tumbling in orbit

Old Friend, Last Whisper

Old Friend, Last Whisper

You lay on the tiny mattress close to the earth
in a room that shone with October light
cumulus mauve and fuchsia drapes, birdsong
interlaced with the graceful melody of harp
a felted orca suspended above your hospice quilt.

I held the air in open palms, shared a poem
heard the passing of hooves—perhaps the roan mare you rode
tempo of raspy neighs and steady heartbeat
arbutus leaves all russet and brittle underfoot
how time is a distant reflection now, the old Franklin stove
chugging its dry kindling for last call
flames flickering, the ache of this day.

Old friend, last whisper—more a sigh, as you push
against the rails of infirmity, cast out a last word
memory now crowning, tumbling in orbit
amber glint of the hummingbird's wing
beyond the open window of this vigil's room.

The phoenix rises in flame, your last river's meander
teal skies, the fields golden for harvest
where the four-legged and winged wait.

The Other is dissimilar to and the opposite of the Self, of Us, and of the Same.
The Oxford Companion to Philosophy

THE OTHER

One

Tell me when it began? An eternity recalls my childhood shadow. The toddler-in-arms could not tell the difference between here and there, returning or wanting to stay.

Did anyone make a diagnosis? I lit up on the x-ray table and medical students swarmed. Barium milkshakes, speculation by omission. My insides turned inside-out.

Where was your mother? They tore her from me, a reversal of birth. Her coat buttons went flying. After that, blue lights from croup tent rooms formed a runway down the corridor. I wandered. I might well have left the building.

What else? Something followed me from behind the walls of that infirmary. It spoke in code, whispered phrases. The repetition dogged me.

What else? Men of the cloth whispered the same phrases. Was I being called up or called down? The voices rolled like the prodrome for thunder. Vertigo's dance, perpetual.

Two

What did you do next? I picked up stones and polished them.
Scribbled verses in tiny journals. I stayed awake
and listened to crickets and owls.
Fell shy of the shoreline and landed in the lake.

I remember that lake. It tempted me. I couldn't swim.
Skated on it instead. Sharp blades, breath like frost,
shoot the duck in long succession. Run. Skate. Run.

Did the whisper-voice follow?
Behind the brick walls of the Maritime house before dawn.
I woke to creaking sounds on the stairs and lost my voice.
A black robe brushing the hardwood floor.
A crone's shadow. Old, bereft, calling.

I bet you wanted to leave. My legs froze.
The crone tied them in knots.
This time the bardo was quicksand.
I could not get up.

Tell me more. Her gaze broke and I woke.
After that my mother placed a blue light in my night room.

Three

Where are you now? I'm gulping oxygen like goldfish at the surface of the pond.

What do you mean? I burned my doll's dress and made her a swimsuit to wear. I named her *Betty Nose,* she was my favourite doll. She had no reason to breathe. She was happy at the bottom of the lake.

Did you change your name? Once. I penciled in Delphina but the blank stares of the teachers haunted me.

Did the cat get your tongue? I preferred growls, hollers, hissing. Feral. I kept words locked up in my journal. One night I spoke in tongues. Echoes came up from the ravine. I ran, skates slung over my shoulder. I dreamed of that frozen lake.

Did you skate in pageants? I was a rabbit with full lop ears, a suit of white fur, whiskers made from pipe cleaners. Then I became the goddess of maize. Demeter on ice. Swaying in arena rows.

I hate to ask. Did the voice return? Up from under the ice. After a hard rain. The glass dome of the lake cracked and whined like the angry wind's whistle. I heard it say: *just this once, step out from your figure-eights.*

Four

*You're not going to believe this. The voice that always whispers
turned up in my dream.* It slithers like a chorus in the middle of a
song. The moonflower feigns sleep after dark. Sea horse silhouettes
glaze the folding petals. I know, I was there. It was Ulrike's wake.

Well now you've lost me, a segue or a maze? The poems shape-shift
just like the corn goddess on skates. The voice appears in lower-case,
between lines. Shows up under the ice.

Are you still afraid? The portents are disguised but always
tell the truth. *Deep menace, ancient argument, a fatal wound.*
That poem followed me home. How the rushing water washed
my trepidation, made me forget the mountain.

You were bridging the white water. I was preparing for winter.
Feeding fire from the earth. Far from the shadow's edge. This
was Haidée's song. Remember?

Run. Skate. Run. If only my ankles could carry me back across
the lake. Centre of gravity fails. Don't grow old.
Tuck the arms in to save energy before the bell-lap sprint.

Five

Still sleep with a blue light? Yes.

I enter along the perimeter counterclockwise,
wave goodbye to the ten thousand faces of chaos
speak the names of the fallen between steps
wash tears as they evaporate to higher altitudes

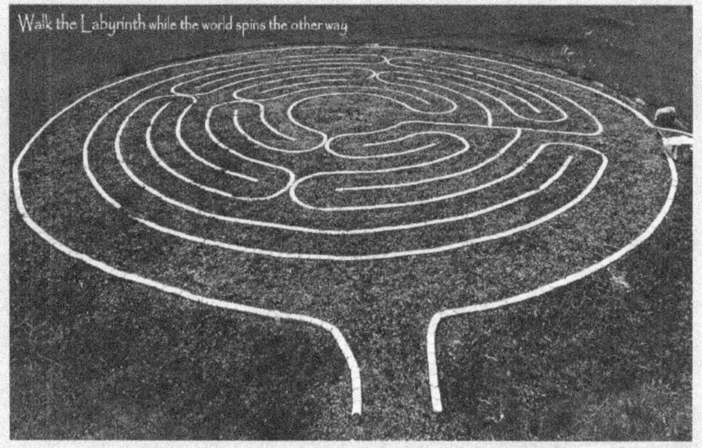

Walk the Labyrinth
While the World Spins the Other Way

I'm walking the community labyrinth
a gift in cemetery fields near Churchill Farm
on an island that holds four decades of my best life—
sea and rock, cedar and shell, rose and kora.

Yarrow carpets the footpath, neat loops and turns
the whole plant good for wound healing and fever
styptic and tenacious, wild perennial
a pungent earthy scent soothing my steps
as I go deeper into my pilgrim wander.

Barefoot, end-of-season bees avoid my feet
this fourth century ritual in slow gait and intention
Today's news and yesterday's dead pass me in cued mirage
going the other way, centuries of turbulent sorrow
baked lands and fossilized tears
infant bones preserved with embroidered shrouds.

Turn, turn again, don't lose that full abandon—
antidote to fear—chants the cantor in my ear
shimmer of medicinal leaves like prayer flags
over the only Celtic cross in the field
highest monument in this half-acre's hollow.
By the time I pass through the twists and easterly turns
I am truly lost, feet following faith's buried compass.

This labyrinth is a replica of Chartres minus two loops
I enter along the perimeter counterclockwise
wave goodbye to the ten thousand faces of chaos
speak the names of the fallen between steps
wash tears as they evaporate to higher altitudes
while the days take their leave and I enter
the soul of the rose.

Climbing Ancestry Trees

You painted your gardens in words, sent blessings in letters.
Come home, you called through pen and ink.
We have much to share these spring mornings.
That year I was seventeen, lost between
Toronto's grey skyline and darkness
       not knowing where I belonged, looking in the wrong places.

We have two magnolias coming into bloom.
Plenty of flowers by the end of the week.
Sammy watches me from the roof of the house.
Tries to inveigle me to help him down to earth.
The other day he came into the house, a butterfly in his mouth.
Dropped it at your mother's feet. She said—
       'I guess the snakes are hidden underneath the lawn.'

How would I know all the miles between Great Lakes—Huron,
past Blind River, Superior with its endless shores—
taking me a week to reach Qu'Appelle in that old driveaway Ford
the stone bridge near the CPR tracks, late day's prairie stretch
where I gathered all the memories you wrote in cards,
       an old barrow's wheel, the stories behind that forged iron.

Rhododendrons are in bloom. I am cultivating around the roots.
The camelia may not make it this year. I planted pinks
       and polyanthus.
I would like to get a tea rose. Tall with citrus scent.
Today I found trollius. Mrs. Compton had one, you might remember.
The hawthorn trees are in leaf on the boulevard,
soon the flowers will show up. Come home.

Now I'm climbing ancestry trees,
looking for your mother's mother.
Four degrees of separation in Cheshire fields and farms.
I've found Eliza, your father's sister. I keep looking, listening.
You speak from these pages, crossing the threshold.
Your handwriting cultivates roots, nourishes the bones.
      Come back. We've got bulbs to plant, roses to prune.

Almost transparent now, I speak
through your pen. Come home
to the memory of wonder.

Memory of Wonder

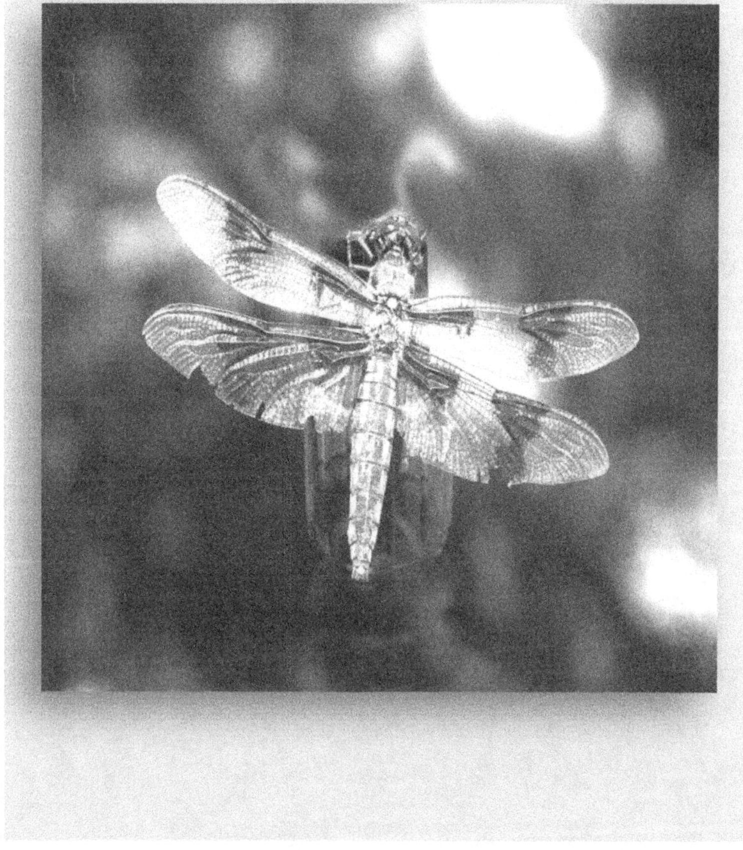

Memory of Wonder   for Molly, in *Annwn*

I see you in the apple trees next to the gabled shed
climbing, always reaching higher
where branches are sparse and leaves are falling.
No fear, just wonder.
Body lithe and supple, nearly taking flight.
The day is bright, the lake calls you.
Are the fish leaping?

We take a walk, wander the Jones Lake Loop
Watch for tadpoles, a loveliness of ladybugs
the yellow tipped tail of a Cedar Waxwing.
Collect rocks of red siltstone, worry them in pockets
all the wily creatures building nests or warrens
tucked up close to the water's edge.

I hold your hand, give you the nudge.
Your poems will spawn this autumn
like the wise salmon of Finn MacCool
eating the magic hazel nuts.

Believing alchemy, divining the day
blue damselfly wings, diaphanous
weave crossveins for lift and aerial view.

Know I will be there in the flowers—
dahlias, hydrangeas, dianthus, pansies.
Grow them bright with sweet and spicy scent.

Your hand now holds this pen—
your poem forms the song.
Sing now, I am not far on the wind.
Finn's eyes shine from the secret pool.

We stand at the nape of falling water
the urge to dive, go further upstream.
Almost transparent now, I speak
through your pen. Come home
to the memory of wonder.

Nourish the last roses blooming at the Equinox. Count petals for the ones that fall last. Tiny velvet robes placed in your altar bowl of blue. Adorn your shawl with Janet's rose oil.

How Do You Spell Joy?

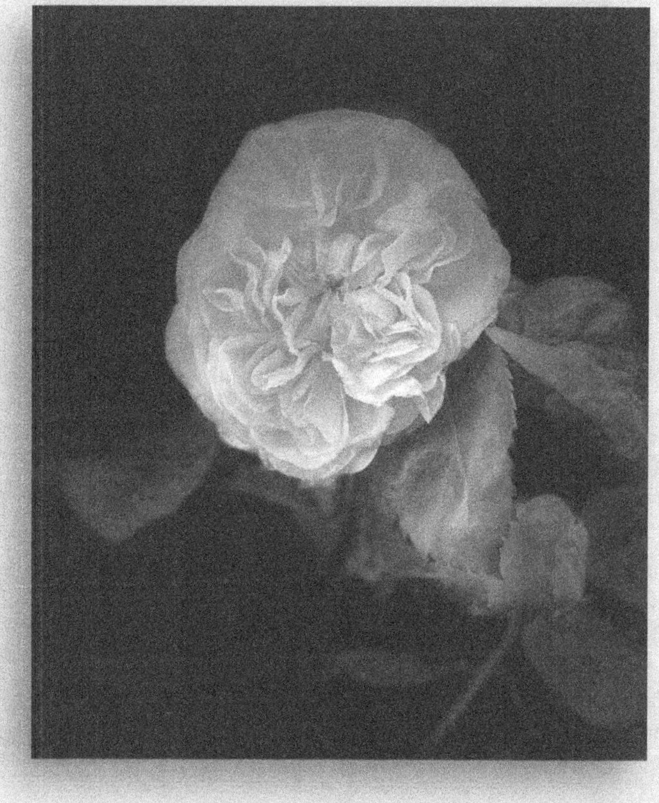

How Do You Spell Joy?

I wish I could show you when you are lonely or in darkness
 the astonishing light of your own being.
> *How did the rose ever open its heart and give to this world*
> *all its Beauty? Love, love, love. This sky where we live*
> *is no place to lose your wings.*   Hafiz

Strip down at the ocean's edge. Never mind who's on the beach.
Mirrors are for dressing rooms. Walk in. Don't hold your breath.
Join the shiners hanging about the bay. Swim strong, taste salt.

Sit up late into the night with that one book that is your deserted-
island choice. Savour words slowly like it's a matter of survival.
Recite and roll the syllables like morsels of your favourite foods.

Call your sisters. Tell them you're flying home tomorrow.
The seaplane will be your seamstress for new wings.
Your fears fall away from the windscreen like cloud droplets.

Nourish the last roses blooming at the Equinox. Count petals
for the ones that fall last. Tiny velvet robes placed in your
altar bowl of blue. Adorn your shawl with Janet's rose oil.

Paint pictures in words for each scent: freesia, sweet olive,
lily of the valley, sweet autumn clematis. Plant your poems
at the headstone of your sorrow. Seed the eternal flame.

Find yourself at Kilmurvey Beach. Walk the length of Inis Mór
fleet of foot. Lay down near the temple stones. Call in Brigid.
Follow her to the holy well.

Listen to *Constantinople's* Montreal concert ten more times.
Slow dance the sixth track, see how pain is the mind's cave,
not the body. Fall in love with the instruments, the grace of
Ablaye's Kora, Kiya's Setar. Singing Hafiz's *Wild Gazelle*.

Count back from ten slowly. Each number arrives with a
special guest. Call them by their birth names: Ocean, Salt,
Swim, Poem, Wings, Stones, Setar, Rose, Holy Well,
Wild Gazelle.

Through kaleidoscopic hues we saw beyond and further
Where hostas bloom their waxy whites in evening sky
Past the timeless gate, then vanish all too soon, under the
            Light of the swan-white moon.

In the Garden with P.K.

In the Garden with P.K.

> *Light of the swan-white moon.*
> *The blazing light of trees.*
> *And the rarely glimpsed bright face*
> *behind the apparency of things.*
>
> P.K. Page, "The Filled Pen" from
> *Evening Dance of the Grey Flies*

All afternoon we reclined on braided lounges of rattan
Your interior garden draped in bougainvillea's magenta
Hibiscus and zinnia hugging the raku pots at our feet.
Green upon green beyond our gaze, plantain lily long-lived
I had not visited such terraced worlds of colour,
except in dreams.
You made iced tea and biscuits, the air
unusually close for June.
Through kaleidoscopic hues we saw beyond and further
Where hostas bloom their waxy whites in evening sky
Past the timeless gate, then vanish all too soon, under the
    Light of the swan-white moon.

We spoke of matters of the heart, wounds without words
The deeper layers barely visible in the fleet days of youth,
Twenty-one that year and my library spare, you shared
Loren Eiseley's *Night Country*, writing of mammoth bones
Pond life teeming in the salt flats of Loren's mid-west
Where magic is always found in water, even alongside
the quays. You brought me to Rumi's *Guest House* and
    The Conference of the Birds,
Gifts that followed into night,
startling infinities of darkness and light
My long journey home, free of the questions' unease,
shining under
    The blazing light of trees.

Was it Brazil where you first flew toward that secret sky? *La ciel*
Or the puzzle mazes, labyrinths, or hedgerows you walked as a child?
Maybe it was orchids in the kapok tree, drums from the favelas
That drove you deeper into green, transmuting colour, where
Insects and suns, caves and water, danced from your filled pen.
For the longest time I was soothed in stillness, your garden's grace.
We sat with memory's palette, mine now sharp as decades past
Olfactory, tactile, infinite shades of parakeet, chartreuse, and sage,
Waiting now for *that shake that heralds a new world*, only a trace
     And the rarely glimpsed bright face.

Eiseley still on my shelves, Coleman's Rumi on the nightstand,
                              your voice
Distilling the rhythms as you write: *never forget the beauty*.
The last time you read from *The Glass Air*, island's winter festival
Wearing turquoise and silver hoops, your cataracts now gone
Miraculously you declared, as if for the first time seeing the
                              secret depths
Of indigo, aromatic porphyrins at the heart, a garden's wellspring
Here and there, now and then, flowing by osmosis back to Brazil
Where the earth shook and you took up pen and ink,
Revealing all that's hidden, *World within World,* translucent wings
     Behind the apparency of things.

Acknowledgements

I gratefully acknowledge the financial assistance of the
DC Reid Poets' Grant from the Writer's Trust of Canada
which allowed me the time to work on this collection.

Some of the poems were shortlisted for the following contests
or appeared in earlier versions in the following books /journals:

This is the Moon's Work, Mother Tongue Publishing
Forcefield (anthology), Mother Tongue Publishing
Poets' Caravan, Planet Earth Poetry
Freefall Magazine Poetry Contest shortlist and finalist,
     2023 and 2025
Royal City Literary Arts Society E-Zine
Pulp Literature Kingfisher Poetry Award
Sapphire and the Hollow Bone, Ekstasis Editions
North Shore Literary Association Literary Contest
Muriel's Journey Poetry Prize, *Fire from the Heart*
The Galway Review
Pinole Poetry
Sublime: Poems for Vanishing Ice (2026)

Clíodna (KLEE-nah), or Cliodhna,
is the Celtic goddess of the sea and the Otherworld.

Jim Harrison's poem "Poet Warning" quoted from *Songs of Unreason,*
2011.

Quotation on the dedication page is from *Beauty: The Invisible
Embrace,* John O'Donohue, Harper Perennial, 2005.

Many thanks to Rhonda Lillard for granting permission
to quote from the poetry of her late husband, Charles Lillard.

Line quoted in "Otter Point Squalls" (stanza 7):
from "The Island Voice" *A Coastal Range,* Charles Lillard,
Sono Nis Press, 1984, and (stanza 9) from "The Third Day of
May," Charles Lillard, private correspondence, 1977.

Closing lines in "Postcards from the Skeena," and epigraph for "Seascape from Sheringham Point" are from *Jabble*, Charles Lillard, Kanchenjunga Press, 1975.

Lines quoted in "Seascape from Sheringham Point" are from *Seamarks*, St.-John Perse, translation by Wallace Fowlie, Harper Torchbooks, 1961.

Lines appearing in "Telegram from Rivers Inlet" are constructed from words or phrases written by Charles Lillard in private correspondence, 1977.

Epigraph for "Hawking the Surf" is from "The Low Sky," in *The Selected Poetry of Robinson Jeffers*, Random House, 1959; lines in italics appearing in stanzas 3 and 7 are from "Tamar," *The Selected Poetry of Robinson Jeffers*.

Epigraph for "Merwin's Mountain" is from "The Mountain," *Green with Beasts*, W.S. Merwin, Rupert Hart-Davis, 1956.

All photographs by Diana Hayes, except her monochrome interpretations of the following images:
Redbird, by H. Horel
Northern Fur Seal, video image by Island Wildlife NCC
Memory of Wonder, by Peter Southam
Labyrinth, by All Saints by-the-Sea, Salt Spring Island

THANK YOU...

— to poets in my Salt Spring writing group who provided
valuable feedback for many of the poems in this collection:
Brian Day, Sandi Johnson, Celia Meade, Karl Meade, Rowan Percy,
Chris Smart, Murray Reiss.

— to Murray Reiss, who copy-edited the manuscript with his
poet's eagle eye.

— to my publisher, Candice James of Silver Bow Publishing, for
believing in this manuscript and bringing the poems and
photographs into the light.

— As always, to my husband, Peter Southam, for his patience
and loving kindness while I tended to the call of those middle-
of-the night poems.

Diana Hayes currently resides on the traditional and unceded territory of the Coast Salish Hul'q'umi'num' and SENĆOŦEN speaking people—what is known as Salt Spring Island BC. She was born in Toronto and has lived on the east and west coasts of Canada. She received her BA (UVIC) and MFA (UBC) in Creative Writing and has published seven books of poetry, most recently *Labyrinth of Green* (Plumleaf Press), *Language of Light* (House of Appleton), and *Sapphire and the Hollow Bone* (Ekstasis Editions) which was a finalist for the Sunshine Coast (SCWES) Poetry Award.

Deeper Into the Forest, a spoken word/music CD, was produced at Allowed Sound Studio in 2020 with musician and sound engineer, Andy Meyers. She has been shortlisted for The Freefall Poetry Contest, the RCLAS Poetry Contest, The Delta Literary Arts Society Short Film Festival, Muriel's Journey Poetry Contest, and she won first place in the North Vancouver Writers' Association Poetry Contest.

Her debut novella, *Looking for Cornelius*, was published fall 2025 by Wipf & Stock/Resource Publications. She launched Raven Chapbooks in 2020 and publishes small edition poetry chapbooks featuring B.C. poets.

Poet's Website: DianaHayes.ca